Magnetic North

Books by Linda Gregerson

Magnetic North

Linda Gregerson

A MARINER BOOK
Houghton Mifflin Company
Boston · New York

First Mariner Books edition 2008
Copyright © 2007 by Linda Gregerson

www.houghtonmifflinbooks.com.

Library of Congress Cataloging-in-Publication Data
Gregerson, Linda.
Magnetic north / Linda Gregerson.
p. cm.
ISBN-13: 978-0-618-71870-2
ISBN-10: 0-618-71870-2
I. Title.
PS3557.R425M34 2007
811'.54 — dc22   2006035476

ISBN: 978-0-547-08576-0 (pbk.)

Printed in the United States of America

Book design by Robert Overholtzer

EB-L 10 9 8 7 6 5 4 3 2

Grateful acknowledgment to the editors of the following publications,
in which these poems first appeared: *Atlantic Monthly:* "Bright Shadow."
Kenyon Review: "Bicameral," "The Burning of Madrid as Seen from
the Terrace of My House," "Prodigal," "Over Easy." *Laurel Review:*
"*De Magnete.*" *New England Review:* "Dido in Darkness," "The
Turning," "The Chapel *Doom.*" *Ploughshares:* "Make-Falcon." *Poetry:*
"Father Mercy, Mother Tongue," "My Father Comes Back from the
Grave," "Sweet," "Spring Snow." *Slate:* "At the Window." *Smartish
Place:* "Another Diana." *TriQuarterly:* "Elegant," "No Lion, No Moon."
"Elegant" was commissioned by the Calouste Gulbenkian Foundation
and published in *Wild Reckoning: An Anthology Provoked by Rachel
Carson's "Silent Spring,"* ed. John Burnside and Maurice Riordan.
London: Calouste Gulbenkian Foundation, 2004. "Make-Falcon" was
adapted by Susan Botti as a composition for voices, harps, piano, and
percussion and was performed as a work-in-progress at the American
Academy in Rome on May 27, 2006. "Bicameral" and "Elegant" were
reprinted in *American Alphabets: Twenty-five Contemporary Poets,* ed.
David Walker. Oberlin, Ohio: Oberlin College Press, 2006, 168–84.

To the University of Michigan's Institute for the Humanities, and
to John Rich, warm gratitude for a fellowship that enabled me to
work for a blessed year on the present volume.

These poems (and their author) have benefited immeasurably from
the friendship of three impeccable and generous readers: David Baker,
Michael Collier, and Rosanna Warren. Bountiful thanks to them
and, always, to Steven.

For my mother,
    Karen Mildred Gregerson

Contents

Magnetic North

Sweet

Linda,
said my mother when the buildings fell,

before, you understand, we knew a thing
    about the reasons or the ways

    and means,
while we were still dumbfounded, still

bereft of likely narratives, *We cannot*
    continue to live in a world where we

    have so much
and other people have so little.

Sweet, he said.
    Your mother's wrong but sweet, the world

    has never self-corrected,
you Americans break my heart.

Our possum — she must be hungry or
    she wouldn't venture out in so

    much daylight — has found
a way to maneuver on top of the snow.

Thin crust. Sometimes her foot breaks through.
    The edge

    of the woods for safety or
for safety's hopeful look-alike. *Di-*

delphis, "double-wombed," which is
    to say, our one marsupial:

    the shelter then
the early birth, then shelter perforce again.

Virginiana for the place. The place
    for a queen

    supposed to have her maidenhead.
He was clever.

He had moved among the powerful.
    Our possum — possessed

    of thirteen teats, or so
my book informs me, quite a ready-made

republic — guides
    her blind and all-but-embryonic

    young to their pouch
by licking a path from the birth canal.

Resourceful, no? Requiring
    commendable limberness, as does

    the part I've seen, the part
where she ferries the juveniles on her back.

Another pair of eyes above
    her shoulder. Sweet. The place

    construed as yet-to-be-written-upon-
by-us.

And many lost. As when
        their numbers exceed the sources of milk

        or when the weaker ones fall
by the wayside. There are

principles at work, no doubt:
        beholding a world of harm, the mind

        will apprehend some bringer-of-harm,
some cause, or course,

that might have been otherwise, had we possessed
        the wit to see.

        Or ruthlessness. Or what? Or heart.
My mother's mistake, if that's

the best the world-as-we've-made-it
        can make of her, hasn't

        much altered with better advice. It's
wholly premise, rather like the crusted snow.

Bicameral

I

Choose any angle you like, she said,
the world is split in two. On one side, health

and dumb good luck (or money, which can pass
for both), and elsewhere . . . well,

they're eight days from the nearest town,
the parents are frightened, they think it's their fault,

the child isn't able to suck. A thing
so easily mended, provided

you have the means. I've always thought it was
odd, this part (my nursing school

embryology), this cleft in the world
that has to happen and has to heal. At first

the first division, then the flood of them, then
the migratory plates that make a palate when

they meet (and meeting, divide
the chambers, food

from air). The suture through which (the upper
lip) we face the world. It falls

a little short sometimes, as courage does.
Bolivia once, in May (I'd volunteer

on my vacations), and the boy was nine.
I know the world has harsher

things, there wasn't a war, there wasn't
malice, I know, but this one

broke me down. They brought him in
with a bag on his head. It was

burlap, I think, or sisal. Jute.
They hadn't so much as cut eyeholes.

2

(Magdalena Abakanowicz)

Because the outer layer (mostly copper
with a bit of zinc) is good for speed

but does too little damage (what
is cleaner in the muzzle — you've begun

to understand — is also cleaner in
the flesh), the British at Dum Dum (Calcutta) devised

an "open nose," through which
the leaden core, on impact, greatly

expands (the lead being softer). Hence
the name. And common enough in Warsaw

decades later (it was 1943), despite
some efforts in The Hague. I don't

remember all of it, he wasn't even German,
but my mother's arm —

that capable arm — was severed at
the shoulder, made (a single

shot) a strange thing altogether.
Meat. I haven't been able since

to think the other way is normal, all
these arms and legs.

This living-in-the-body-but-not-of-it.

    3

Sisal, lambswool, horsehair, hemp.
The weaver and her coat-of-many-

harrowings. If fiber found *in situ*, in
agave, say, the living cells that drink

and turn the sun to exoskeleton,
is taken from the body that

in part it constitutes (the
succulent or mammal and its ex-

quisite osmotics), is
then carded, cut, dissevered

in one fashion or another from
the family of origin, and

gathered on a loom,
the body it becomes will ever

bind it to the human and a trail
of woe. Or so

the garment argues. These
were hung as in an abattoir.

Immense (12 feet and more from upper
cables to the lowest hem). And vascular,

slit, with labial
protrusions, skeins of fabric like

intestines on the gallery floor.
And beautiful, you understand.

As though a tribe of intimates (the
coronary plexus, said the weaver) had

been summoned (even such
a thing the surgeon sometimes has

to stitch) to tell us, not unkindly, See,
the world you have to live in is

the world that you have made.

Spring Snow

A kind of counter-
blossoming, diversionary,

doomed, and like
the needle with its drop

of blood a little
too transparently in

love with doom, takes
issue with the season: Not

(the serviceberry bright
with explanation) not

(the redbed unspooling
its silks) I know I've read

the book but not (the lilac,
the larch) quite yet, I still

have one more card to
play. Behold

a six-hour wonder: six
new inches bedecking the

railing, the bench, the top
of the circular table like

a risen cake. The saplings
made (who little thought

what beauty weighs) to bow
before their elders.

The moment bears more
than the usual signs of its own

demise, but isn't that
the bravery? Built

on nothing but the self-
same knots of air

and ice. Already
the lip of it riddled

with flaws, a sort
of vascular lesion that

betokens — what? betokens
the gathering return

to elementals. (She
was frightened

for a minute, who had
planned to be so calm.)

A dripline scoring
the edge of the walk.

The cotton batting blown
against the screen begun

to pill and molt. (Who
clothed them out of

mercy in the skins
of beasts.) And even

as the last of the
lightness continues

to fall, the seepage
underneath has gained

momentum. (So that
there must have been a

death before
the death we call the

first or what became
of them, the ones

whose skins were taken.)
Now the more-

of-casting-backward-than-of-
forward part, which must

have happened while I wasn't
looking or was looking

at the skinning knives. I think
I'll call this mercy too.

Make-Falcon

Frederick II of Hohenstaufen, *The Art of Falconry*

I

Of the oil gland . . . Of the down . . .
             Of the numbers and arrangement
of feathers in the wing . . . I have seen
                    on the plains of Apulia

how the birds in earliest spring were weak
             and scarcely able to fly.
Of the avian nostrils and mandibles . . . Of
                    the regular sequence of molt . . .

Aristotle, apt to credit hearsay where
             experiment alone
can be relied upon, was wrong about
                    the migrant column. Concerning

the methods of capture . . . the jesses . . .
             The swivel, the hood, the falcon's bell . . .

2

The finest of them — here I mean
                    for swiftness, strength,

audacity and stamina — are brooded
             on the Hyperborean cliffs (an island
chiefly made of ice). And I
                    am told but have not ascertained

the farther from the sea they nest,
        the nobler will be the offspring.

   3

Triangular needles are not to be used.
        The room

to be darkened, the bird
        held close in the hands of the assistant,
linen thread. By no means pierce
        the *membrana nictitans,* lying between

the eyeball and the outermost
        tissue, nor place the suture, lest it tear,
too near the edge. To seel,
        from *cilium,* lower lid,

which makes her more compliant to the falconer's
        will but also (I have
seen this in the lesser birds as well) more bold
        in flight. The senses

to be trained in isolation: taste,
        then touch, then hearing (so
the bars of a song she will evermore link to
        food), and then the sight restored,

in order that the falcon may
        be partly weaned or disengaged from that
which comes by nature.
        The falconer's purse or

carneria, owing
  to the meat it holds . . .
The carrier's arm . . . the gauntlet . . . the horse . . .
    They greatly dislike the human face.

  4

If you ask why the train is made of a hare,
    you must know no other flight
more resembles
    the flight at a crane than that

the falcon learns in pursuit of a hare
    nor is more beautiful.
Make-falcon: meaning
    the one who is willing

to fly in a cast with another less
    expert (the seasons
best suited . . . the weather . . . the hours . . .)
    and by example teach.

  5

The removal of dogs, which praise
    will better effect than will the harshest
threats, from the prey. Their reward.
    You must open

the breast and extract the organ that moves
    by itself, which is to say, the heart,
and let the falcon feed.
    The sultan

has sent me a fine machine combining
　　　　　the motions of sun and moon,
and Giacomo makes a poem of fourteen
　　　　　　　lines. The music is very good,

I think. (Of those who refuse to come to the lure . . . Of
　　　　　shirkers . . . Of bating . . .)
But give me the falcon for art.

Bright Shadow

for Peter Davison

Wherever they come from whether the all-
        but-impenetrable bracken
                on the nearer
        side of Maple Road (so closely does she bed

them down) or deeper in the wetland (each
        new season surrendering further to
                the strangle
      of purple loosestrife) they

have made for weeks a daybed of
        the longer
                grass beneath the net
      that sometimes of an evening marks

the compass of our shuttlecock
        so Steven
                when at last he finds
      an afternoon for mowing must purposely

chase them into the woods where she
        so watchful
                in the normal course of foraging but
      lulled or made a stranger to her own

first-order instinct for dis-
        quietude (so firmly
                have the scents and apparitions of
      this people-riddled bit of earth impressed

themselves upon the wax that stands for world-
                as-usual) (a scant
                                twelve months ago she was
                herself the sucking diligence that made

the mother stagger on the dew-drenched
                lawn) will find them near the salt lick and
                                as by a subtle field-of-
                force will reel them back to

stations-of-the-daily-path that portion out
                their wakefulness
                                (the ravaged
                rhododendrons bearing witness) forever en-

grafting the strictures of hunger (bright shoots)
                to the strictures (bright
                                shadow) of praise.

The Burning of Madrid as
Seen from the Terrace of My House

Juan Muñoz, sculptor, 1953–2001

Sometime later or maybe just before,

I mentioned I'd been reading on the bus
that very morning while returning from

the Nymphenburg . . .

though now that I consider it I think
it must have been a tram or else

I'd caught a glimpse of the rails, something odd

about the stop . . . yes
it must have been a tram. I mentioned

that the architect, having come

to court at the age of eleven, had been taught —
the Elector of Bavaria had seen

that he'd been taught — mathematics, engineering,

and (later in Paris) the art of Rococo,
though I hadn't yet learned about the

books: paneling, wrought-iron work,

the problematic ceilings, chairs.
Fifty-five volumes in eighteen years . . .

(The Prompter,
1989)*

17

I happened at about that time

to mention that the architect — he'd come
to court on the strength of it as they

did sometimes — had also been a dwarf . . .

       ✦

Sharp as a pen, who said that? About
somebody's nose, that is, portending

death . . . the arches of the feet, the knees,

and how-had-I-even-so-briefly-forgotten upward
and upward, cold (a tide) as any stone.   (*Conversation
                                                            Pieces, I–V,* 1991)

The sculptor appears to have come to a similar

thought by way of a (resin for the models,
bronze) by way (you remember

the clowns we had? — in-

flatable, weighted
at the bottom, you could punch them and

they'd stand back up) by way of a different

regression.
The figures, five of them, mired

in the very means of locomotion, hemi-

spheric bases (half
a world) that elsewhere

might signify play but here

(of resin-textured bronze, remember) ball
and chain. Identical

noses (sharp), barred eyes.

As the newborn, slick with meconium . . . as
the body's exudations in a fever-

fashioned sleep will crust . . .

It was winter, I think, there were
cinders on the museum steps, a margin of ice

on the lake, but I may be misremembering.

As though the eyes
had been pasted shut then opened and

the milky integument hardened to bronze.

✦

A dwarf, he said. And built
the place.

The audience chambers, lobbies, arcades: there was

none of it meant to be private as we latterly
construe the term.

I've given him in the present installation   (*The Prompter,*
      1988)

something akin to it, so
I like to think, akin

to the place (the Archi-

medean point) the court
reserved for its best misfits.

See?

The elevated floor (parquet),
the whiff of proscenium, vanishing point . . .

and down by the footlights the

prompter's box. Observe
how only he — the dwarf — can be said

to have his feet on the ground. The

actors are thinking (stalled,
unmoored except for him) there were lines

they'd been meant to say.

       ◆

. . . to . . . ?

       ◆

   Skin of our teeth.
Why gloves? Why cotton coverings for the feet?

The Cirque Fernando (1879, Degas)

as reenacted later in a holding cell.
Allow me

an image, the bureaucrat says, I'm out   (*Hanging Figure,*
                                                1997)
on a limb here my PowerPoint's stuck. Allow me
Miss Lala (Degas, pastel) against

a background of green and orange. Perhaps

she was born in Africa (observe
the hair, observe

the artist's rendering of her thrown-back head),

the people have paid to see her just
as we do here: triumphantly

above them, strong, the involuted ruching on her

costume so extravagant (the seamstress
ever on call and cheap) it might

be icing on pastry, and (and here's

the point)
and in her mouth the rope.

I think

we are meant to feel in the present instance that
(in place of the costume, a uniform, in place

of the vibrant color, gray: as much

a common hanging as a circus act) I
think we are meant to understand we aren't

ourselves quite off the hook. (Or else

I'd caught a glimpse of the rails. It was winter. It was
standard-issue everything.) The others

had had their feet cut off. For scale.

✦

Which brings us . . . ?

✦

Which brings us back to the prompter, who

has built a city of balsa wood.
What would you say the scale is here? The

miniature awnings, blinds,

the pavements cleared of every anecdotal
bit of business. Won't

*(The Burning of
Madrid as Seen
from the Terrace
of My House,* 1999)

the stagehands be surprised when they return

from break.
You see the little balconies?

How easily they burn?

Father Mercy, Mother Tongue

If the English language was good enough for Jesus
            Christ, opined
      the governor of our then-most-populous

            state, *it is good enough for the schoolchildren*
                  of Texas.
      Which is why, said the man at the piano, I

will always love America: the pure
            products
      of the Reformation go a little crazy here.

                  Red bowl
                  of dust, correct us, we
            are here on sufferance every one.

   In 1935 the very earth rose up
                  against us, neither
            tub-soaked sheets nor purer thoughts could keep it

out. Doorsills, floorboards, nostrils,
                  tongue. The sugarbowl
            was red with it, the very words we spoke

            were dirt.
      There must have been something
                  to do, said my youngest one once (this
      was worlds
                  away and after the fact).

We hoped for rain.

We harvested thistle to feed the cows.
We dug up soapweed. Then
we watched the cows and pigs and chickens die. *Red*
bowl

of words.

And found ourselves as nameless as
those poor souls up from Mexico

and just about as welcome as the dust.
Pity the traveler
camping by a drainage ditch in someone else's

beanfield, picking someone else's bean crop *who is here*
and gone.

And look

where all that parsing of the Latin led: plain Eunice
in her later years refused

to set foot in a purpose-
built church (a cross
may be an idol so
a white-
washed wall may be one too), preferring to trust

a makeshift circle of chairs in the parlor
(*harbor for*
the heart in its simplicity),
her book.

This morning
I watched a man in Nacogdoches calling
all of the people to quit

24

their old lives, there were screens
within screens: the one

above his pulpit (so huge
was the crowd), the one I worked
with my remote. *Then turn . . .*

And something like the vastness of the parking lot
through which
they must have come (so
huge) appeared
to be on offer, something

shimmered like the tarmac on an August day.

Is this
the promised solvent? (some were
weeping, they were black and white).

A word

so broad and shallow (*Flee*), so rinsed
of all particulars (*Flee Babel,*

said the preacher) that translation's
moot. The tarmac
keeps the dust down, you must give it

that. The earth this time will have to scrape us off.

At the Window

Suppose, we said, that the tumult of the flesh
were to cease
and all that thoughts can conceive, of earth,
of water, and of
air, should no longer speak to us; suppose
that the heavens
and even our own souls were silent, no longer
thinking of themselves
but passing beyond; suppose that our dreams
and the visions
of our imagination spoke no more and that every
tongue and every sign
and all that is transient grew silent — for all
these things
have the same message to tell, if only we can
hear it, and
their message is this: We did not make ourselves,
but he
who abides forever made us. Suppose, we said,
that after giving
us this message and bidding us listen to him who
made them they
fell silent and he alone should speak to us,
not through them
but in his own voice, so that we should hear
him speaking,
not by any tongue of the flesh or by an angel's
voice, not in the
sound of thunder or in some veiled parable
but in his own voice,
the voice of the one for whose sake we love
what he has made;

suppose we heard him without these, as we two
strained to do . . .

And then my mother said, "I do not know why
I am here."
And my brother for her sake wished she might
die in her own
country and not abroad and she said, "See
how he speaks."
And so in the ninth day of her illness, in the
fifty-sixth year
of her life and the thirty-third of mine, at the
mouth of the Tiber
                    in Ostia . . .

The Chapel *Doom*

Where once the risen body
stood, one hand held aloft
in judgment, one hand not, in

judgment too, where once
the newly wakened dead were
drawn as to a compass point,

where even now the ghostly
trace of pigment-laden plaster
marks a firmament that

quarried stone might vainly
seek to emulate, to which
the stone is nothing but

a bar of sand, there would,
if he were once
to take on flesh again

as hourly was expected, be
no room now, they
have cut the wall, in

deference to the ceiling
and its fourfold modern
moldings, white

on white, so short.
"It's faded," said
the only other person there.

And I with my pittance
of history: "This must
have been all that was

left." "I mean,"
he said (and what
had I thought? — that

no one else remembered
the quarrel? — whitewash
then in calmer times the

whitewash stripped), "I
mean these fifty years,"
he said, "I used

to go to school here, I
had nothing else to look at
during morning prayers."

The durable stain,
the one that gained most deeply
on the porous stone before

the faithful suffered their
change of heart, the one
that makes a present

backdrop for the featureless
creatures in silhouette, the
damned, whom demons drag

to torment, also the saved,
still stunned, whose empty
faces lift toward emptiness

above them, this
most stubborn impregnation
of the found world by the

made, is green. Which my
books say was not a color
friendly to the painter then.

Time's mineral
collusions mean
to make us wrong. So what

shall we make of the city
surviving in so much
detail? In traceries,

towers, in crowded ranks
of gabled roofs, in bays
and corbels, spandrels light

as masons could contrive or
mind imagine: this
is not a city built for siege,

the very crenelations have
no purpose but to please
the eye. A city

in a chapel in a market
town where once
the playwright's father (these

were flush years, he was
chamberlain) among
his civic duties oversaw

the painting-over that
secured the state. God's
city saved from dryrot and

the hardwood-chewing
beetle, from forgetfulness
and fallings-out, from even

that amendment which
has left no room
for god's return. The ceiling

white. So whitely
does the vaulting turn the
light away it seems to have

no planes at all and thus
no explanation but the one,
the keeping weather

out. It must
be in some other life we
fill the rooms with people.

The Turning

Just then, when already he's trying
        to leave, improbably

        young and fair-
complected, the absence of pigment a kind

of disease — he's come as a last
        concession and the church

        is cold, the other,
the pastor, so palpably wedded to grief he

looks with envy at the fair one, grief's
        addictive, it will hitch

        a ride on anything —
and that's when it happens, off-camera,

outside, some parting of the beaten
        sky as relayed

        by the gaffer, and
the window for a moment floods with not

that winter light from which the film, in English,
        takes its name but

        winter scorched
by heaven's high contempt so that

the simplest among us may see and under-
        stand: no help.

You dreary
Scandinavians, my husband says, your

serotonin uptake goes awry and you decide
        it's metaphysical.

        But isn't (I'll grant
the serotonin) isn't that just the point?

The cameraman makes his meticulous
        case for the folds

        of an eyelid, the decent
proportion of table and chair, the un-

remitting body of the world in all
        its loveliness, and still

        the one who suffers is
determined to be lost. He'd gladly

sell his unborn child for one decisive
        scourging if

        it meant
the one-who-scourges were for just

that instant forced to show his hand.
        He's hopelessly

        outmatched, of course,
the god of irony has such a long head start.

And therefore I think he stands for us,
        the pallid one, though he

believes and we do not.
Though he has been punished once

for believing and once for despair, while we
       confine our scruple to

       the mise en scène.
He's all but gone. He will not live to see

another suppertime, the one
       who was to be

       his lifeline hasn't
any life to spare. And so he turns

but barely, just the slightest
       movement sideways

       of his eyes, as though
to spare the one, the man

of God, whose monstrous self-absorption is
       as lethal as a loaded

       gun, to spare him his own
iniquity. The turning

is a kind of tact, you see it still in
       country people,

       my uncle when
he visits always sits near the door so his boots

won't soil the kitchen. First
        the scorching then

        — the faithful
have a name for this — the ordinary cold.

De Magnete

I

The lodestone; what it is.
    Which pole is the north; how the north
pole is distinguished from the south.
    What iron is; what its matter, its use.
That the earth herself is magnetic and
    by reason of these potencies
lies ever in the same direction. Of
    magnetic coition. Of axis and poles.
Of motion produced by magnets though
    through solid bodies interposed.
That the love of iron and lodestone
    is greater than that of lodestone and
lodestone or iron and iron when near
    a lodestone and within its field.
Of bodies mutually repellent.
    Of disagreements between pieces
of iron on a single pole of the lodestone.
    Of the mariner's compass. Of longitude.
Of variation under the equinoctial
    line. That the formal
magnetic act is spherically effused.
    That the earth hath a circular motion.
Arguments of those who deny this
    motion, and refutation thereof.
Anomaly in the equinox; obliquity
    of the celestial sphere. Of diurnal
revolution and the cause of its definite
    time. Of time. That magnetic force
is animate, or imitates a soul.

2

It was during the siege of Lucera
    that Petrus Peregrinus (Peter
the Pilgrim), builder of catapults, layer
of mines, chief engineer and servant
    to Charles the servant of God,
conducted in his leisure hours behind
    the fortifications whose
erection he himself had lately overseen
    experiments on the lodestone.
From his letter "On the Magnet" (August
    8, 1269), a world
of usefulness and chiefly as to method, only
    later named and codified. "My dearest
friend," he wrote. The scorching wind.
    The city not yet fallen. Soon.

3

As to the ancients, forever ringing
    changes on a few trite truths,
supinely inattentive to the elements
    before them . . . As to the
schoolmen—grammatists, sophists,
    lettered clowns—they
stray about in darkness like a
    rabble. To the fathers of
philosophy, due honor rendered
    ever. But give me
our general mother the earth.

4

Thus William Gilbert, English-
man, his treatise "On the Magnet"
        (1600): *not the polestar, not
an island but the earth herself.* The new
        cosmology partnered at last
by a physics worth the name. "He was
        of stature tall, complexion
cheerful, a happiness quite uncommon
        in so hard a student." "Great,"
wrote Galileo, "to a point that one
        might envy." *I have fashioned
for the purpose of experiment a rounded
        stone.* Terrella, little earth. *Whose
poles* . . . With ardour and unwearied
        application . . . *We must
ever consult the evidence of the eye.*

5

Which evidence the mariners had
by then amassed aplenty. That
        the two, to begin with, the north
we can steer by and the north we call the
        true, diverge, as witness
the logbooks and the solar clocks.
        So Edmund Halley the soap-
boiler's son ("If a star were misplaced
        he would at once be sure
to find it") took the matter up.
        His ship was called the *Paramore*
(two years at sea), his blazon
        to the body of the loved one was

a Map, the first, of Deviation.
    Nailed it. But
("the Svalbard archipelago, a little
    north") the triumph of lovers was ever
short-lived: the pole, it seems,
    is peregrine. Does not stay put.

6

To the College of Physicians (William
    Gilbert again) *all the books*
in my library, my instruments, my globes.
    And wintering on the pack-ice
centuries later, the Norwegian and
    his photographic plates: her current
habitus. "Like hunting a ghost
    in the tundra." Like (*is animate*)
a soul. Her traces describing (we
    can read the data backward) rough
parabolas (*so even in the deepest night*),
    the pole now drifting toward us,
now away (*and thickest weather*), lately
    gaining speed. *Did not*
the earth revolve, the sun would ever
    hang above a single part,
reducing its substance to grievous
    harm, the other parts all cold,
and as the earth herself cannot
    endure so pitiable a prospect, so
she seeks and seeks the sun again,
    turns from him, follows
with her astral mind ("On purpose
    never married") *lest in diverse ways*

she perish ("much renowned") *and be*
    destroyed. The books? *Is it*
likely that the heavens and all the
    spheres, if spheres there be,
should be made to revolve for the sake
    of the earth when the earth
Were lost to fire *can make*
    a motion of herself and for her own
behoof? Were lost unless of course
    you count the one.

Another Diana

Whom we love for her luminous
                    frailties, quite
unlike the goddess for whom she was named.
     Diana

leaks, it's half her charm.
                    The Great Wall Plastic
Factory in Kowloon preferred
     to ship her by the gross — she was

a giveaway at county fairs — and now
                    her small
survivals pass from hand to hand on eBay,
     she

is something of a minor cult. Her
                    plastic body: best
to bring your duct tape. Her disarming
     plastic lens:

a rapid falling-off outside the sweet
                    spot makes
our window on the risen world, in silver
     salts

and gelatin emulsion, seem
                    forever unstable and
partisan: look. Look with
     me at the picture on my wall while I

adjust the light. You see the child?
                    You see

the faded madras of her smock? Her arms
thrown wide as in a

dance, her face . . . But later
                    for the face, I
wonder first if you can help me with the
field, I'm told

they're sugar beets, isn't that
                    slightly odd?
That they should need protection from the
crows? Unless

embarked on her vigil at seedtime she
                    has since, presiding
spirit, kept her arms aloft for simple
joy. The sack-

and-stuffing gathered to make her face — old
                    burlap — falls
a little forward at the ear which
makes no

sense wrong place wrong
                    idiom altogether still
decidedly
        an ear. And then (the plastic

lens) the fade: what in
                    the clearing shines
so fat and proud (the corrugated beet-
crop) quickly

loosens to a kind of fog. How little
                    we seem to require: the one
who sees, the one who, eyeless, dances, passing
        for the human while we talk.

No Lion, No Moon

Štepán Pollack, 1931–1943

But there she is, fair
Thisby, twice: the once

in dirndl and embroidered
blouse, then letter

by letter — *Tisbe* — on
the wall above. Heart-

with-arrow glossing the
name, the heroine's

affliction, and, by
consequence, her claim

on us. Cheap paper, much
yellowed these sixty

years, the crayon
wielded not so much

with art as with
the art of open-

heartedness. Which makes
me think her lover, himself

so easily undone
by words and by

an open heart, un-
likely to have scorned

the hand that formed
the letters mis-

proclaiming *Priam*
just above his head.

What's Pyramus to you,
child? Or you

and all Theresienstadt
to Thisby?

That someone
had the wherewithal

to find the children
crayons at all or guide

them through theatricals,
that someone — not

just someone but the
sum of them, the common-

weal, inside this un-
familiar and malignant

place, this "camp" — could find
the heart to care for

pictures, plays-
within-a-play, and inju-

dicious lovers long
before their keepers

thought to use such things
as camouflage (the Red

Cross sent observers
once) and, caring

for such things, to
make of them something

like a nursery for
the yet-to-be-ex-

terminated soul
of central Europe is

a knot not even
malice on the grand

scale has dissolved.
Thisby knows

so little of the world
as yet: the bit

she can see through the
chink in the wall

has made her heart beat
faster in its cage. But

little as she
knows, she knows

the one thing, there
are forms for this,

his eyes will be like . . .
lips like . . . she is not

required, no more
than the guards

who have loaded the trains,
to make the whole thing up

from scratch. The transcript
and that stubborn other

thing that gets trans-
scription slightly wrong, if only

rarely in our favor. Young
Štepán left the lion out.

My Father Comes Back from the Grave

for Karen

I think you must contrive to turn this stone
        on your spirit to lightness.

        Ten years.
And you, among all the things of the earth he took

to heart — they weren't so many after all — bent nearly
        to breaking with daily

        griefs. *The grass
beneath our feet.* Poor blades. So

leaned on for their wavering homiletic (pressed for
        paltry, perpetual,

        raiment, return,
the *look-for-me* every child appends to absence) it's

a wonder they keep their hold on green. *Come back
        to me as grass beneath*

        my feet. But he
inclined to different metaphors.

        ✦

                Your neighbor,

the young one, the one with two small boys, the one
        who knew

what to do when the
gelding had foundered and everyone else was sick

with fear, can no longer manage the stairs on his own.
The wayward

cells (proliferant,
apt) have so enveloped the brain stem that

his legs forget their limberness. The one
intelligence

driving it all. The one
adaptable will-to-be-ever-unfolding that recklessly

weaned us from oblivion will
as recklessly have done

with us. *Shall the fireweed
lament the fire-eaten meadow?* Nothing

in nature (*whose roots make a nursery of ash*) (but
we . . .) so

parses its days in dread.

✦

And in that other thing,   distinguishing

the species that augments itself with tools.
With

drill bits in
the present case, with hammer, saw,

and pressure-treated two-by-eights: a ramp
          for the chair

             that wheels the one
who cannot walk. He will not live to use

it much, a month perhaps, but that
          part, o

             my carpenter, you
have never stooped to reckon. Now

the father, where does he come in? Whose
          cigarette,

             whose shot glass, whose
broad counsel at the table saw ("I told

you not to do that") ever
          freighted a daughter's learning.

          Whose work
was the world of broken things and a principle

meant to be plain. The grass is mown? The people
          in the house may hold

             their heads up. Not?
A lengthening reproach. And thus

the shadow to your every move. The cough,
          the catch, continuo: the engine

             that breaches your scant four hours
of sleep. And what should you see (still

sleeping) as you look for the source of the sound?
Our father on the mower making

modest assault
on the ever-inadequate-hours-of-the-day, as

manifest in your neglected
lawn. Fed up, no doubt. Confirmed

in his private opinions. But
knightly in his fashion and — it's this

I want to make you see —
in heaven to be called upon.

Over Easy

Cloud cover like a lid on.
        Thwarted trees. And three more hours
of highway to be rid of. My darlings don't want
        a book on tape. They want

a little indie rock, they want to melt
        the tweeters, they want
mama in the trunk so they can have some un-
        remarked-on fun.

Fine. I've got my window, I can contemplate
        the flatness of Ohio. I can think
about the ghastly things we've leached into
        the topsoil, I can marvel that the

scabrous fields will still accept the plow. Except
        some liquid thing is happening just behind
the trees, some narrow sub-
        cutaneous infusion where

the darkening earth and darker strato-
        cumulus have not yet sealed
their hold. A pooling
        fed by needle drip: pellucid, orange,

a tincture I would almost call unnatural were
        it not so plainly nature-
born. Till what had been a stricken contiguity
        of winter-wasted

saplings starts to sharpen and distill, as though
        a lens had been adjusted or a mind

had cleared. *Our sorry dispersal,*
                the Bishop of Africa wrote

to his flock, *but the voice of a child*
          recalled me. When the girls were small
we took them to an island once, the sun
              above the sea, and with

the other paying customers we'd watch it set.
          A yolk, I thought. The not-yet-
torn meniscus with its cunning corrective to
              up and down. You've held

one in your palm no doubt: remember the weight?
          Remember the lemony slickness we so oddly
call "the white" and how it drains
              between your fingers? *Not*

in chambering and wantonness the sun would swell
          nor strife and plumply flatten like
a yolk-in-hand. Would steep there in the salt-
              besotted vapors till

we must have been watching an aftereffect,
          so quickly did it vanish. *Till*
the whole of expectation, wrote the bishop — this
              Ohio sky, the road, my noisy

darlings — *is exhausted and* —
          now mandarin, madder — *what was*
the future — cinnabar, saffron, marigold,
              quince — *becomes the past.*

Prodigal

Copper and ginger, the plentiful
    mass of it bound, half loosed, and
        bound again in lavish

    disregard as though such heaping up
were a thing indifferent, surfeit from
        the table of the gods, who do

        not give a thought to fairness, no,
    who throw their bounty in a single
lap. The chipped enamel — blue — on her nails.

The lashes sticky with sunlight. You would
    swear she hadn't a thought in her head
        except for her buttermilk waffle and

    its just proportion of jam. But while
she laughs and chews, half singing
    with the lyrics on the radio, half

        shrugging out of her bathrobe in the
    kitchen warmth, she doesn't quite
complete the last part, one of the

sleeves — as though, you'd swear, she
    couldn't be bothered — still covers
        her arm. Which means you do not

    see the cuts. Girls of an age —
fifteen for example — still bearing
        the traces of when-they-were-

new, of when-the-breasts-had-not-
been-thought-of, when-the-troublesome-
cleft-was-smooth, are anchored

on a faultline, it's a wonder they
survive at all. This ginger-haired
darling isn't one of my own, if

own is ever the way to put it, but
I've known her since her heart could still
be seen at work beneath

the fontanelles. Her skin
was almost otherworldly, touch
so silken it seemed another kind

of sight, a subtler
boundary than obtains for all
the rest of us, though ordinary

mortals bear some remnant too,
consider the loved one's fine-
grained inner arm. And so

it's there, from wrist to
elbow, that she cuts. She takes
her scissors to that perfect page, she's good,

she isn't stupid, she can see that we
who are children of plenty have no
excuse for suffering we

should be ashamed and so she is
and so she has produced this many-
layered hieroglyphic, channels

raw, half healed, reopened
　　before the healing gains momentum, she
has taken for her copy-text the very

cogs and wheels of time. *And as for*
　　her other body, says the plainsong
　　　　on the morning news, *the hole*

　　in the ozone, the fish in the sea,
you were thinking what exactly? You
　　were thinking a comfortable

　　breakfast would help? I think
I thought we'd deal with that tomorrow.
Then you'll have to think again.

Dido in Darkness

The place had been a chapel once and later
        a sort of hostel for men with no-

        where else to live — You've had your
dinner, yes? You didn't get caught

in the rain? — and then, which seems
        to be matter-of-course in all

        these ventures at goodness, they ran
flat out of money so the lease had lapsed

and hence our play. Our site-specific
        Dido since the site was free.

                                So stairwells, rooftop, chancel-and-
                                nave, the light draining out of the sky

                        on its own, sans dimmer switch, sans
                        tech crew.

        For which the playwright ought
to go down on his knees in thanks and

might if he weren't dead, this one
        so rarely comes up for air.

                                        . . . the queen
                        of Carthage ripe for rescuing.

I bullied them into letting me sing — why
        not? — those lovely fifties songs:

Cupid knows neither time nor place
that can't be turned to purpose. And

it's part of what you paid for, no? Like finding
    yourselves so herded about. You like

    the inconvenience.

                              They've
                contrived the storm with watering cans,

          the cave with casement windows where
              her fate is sealed, if fate

              is not too grand a word for so
          much tawdry scheming. Not

          the stage effects, you understand.
              I mean the tawdry gods.

You like how hard it was to find us.

          What I couldn't quite imagine was how
              they'd manage to do

    So Cupid in lipstick . . .

                              the pyre.

. . . and in a swank if slightly dated . . .

          Tux. Not one thing nor the other. Trans-
          urbanity. If cities

          are built on rubble, which they are,
          and if this violence done to the heart

is merely practice for the other sort (to
some hearts more than others too),

she dies by water as well as fire.

We managed the heaping up quite well:
the rigging, the oars,

the things that should have kept him here,

and then we were nearly
stymied.
Until?

Till someone brought the pitcher in.

She douses the rigging. She douses
the oars. She kneels and with

the cup of her hand begins to bathe
her shoulders, we can almost smell

the kerosene.

A temporal trespass?

A temporal trespass de-
liberate because we're most

convinced by that which most
requires our help. What ought to be oil

and viscous is both water (now
she lifts the vessel, now) both water

and fire, or something infinitely
near to fire, fire-hungry, fire-enabling

(now she pours it on her head
and arms)

while you
in your makeshift pews and I in the

wings with my cigarette

while we inhale
the fumes of empire

But she gets to speak.

the briny solvent

Then she gets to speak:

She says *the darkness gladly.*

Then?

And then she blows the candle out.

And then she blows the candle out.

Elegant

C. elegans

Dewpoint and a level field. Or slick
      of agar,

   microscope,
         the embryonic roundworm and
an open mind. The world so rarely

            lets us in, let's
            praise

   the lucky vista when it does.
          We knew,
said my tutor, that death was a part of it, think

   of the webbing that's eaten away in
            order
          that you may have fingers. We

            didn't know — how to put this? — before

   we mapped our soil-borne roundworm, *C.*

      for *Caenor-* (filth) *hab-*
ditis (one who dwells there) with

its thousand and ninety invariant
            cells of which
      131 and always
   the same

and always in a particular sequence are programmed
for extinction,
                    we had no idea how close
                to the heart of it death
                                        must be.
        At first
                a sort of cratered field, or
                                    granulated — see it? — both

        the raised parts and con-
                            cavities, the sculpting
                                            light,

and then a sort of swelling (it's a corpse now) then
                        engulfment (that's
                the sister cell) and then

                                    the disappearance (you'll
                    remember how the lipids "lose their place").

    And on our chart an *x* where would

                    be daughter cells, "a fate
                        like any other." It's

a lie, of course, the light

        and shadow so disposed, a
                            friendly
        lie, *as if* as in a play: of

                    something less congenial to the seeing

            eye, the microscope
                    makes shadow and

our question gains some traction and the world,

                                        though not
                        just yet and not
                                so seamlessly, makes sense.

Proprietary sequencing? Don't
        break my heart.

                        We thought at first a camera
                would be just the thing, the thing itself in real
                                        time caught for anyone

        to stop
and start, but that

                        was to ignore how much the camera
                misses, how what we call seeing

                                in an ever-changing depth

                of field while (twofold,
                        threefold, turning on its axis, still

        unhatched) our worm

                        performs its complex cleavages and differentiations
                                        is already
                        to have balanced on the scales

of thought. What
                answered, what
        the optics (see Nomarski) really
                                needed on the other end

was homely as the worm: a pencil,

paper, one man preternat-
                                               urally good at this, and
                              thirteen hours,
                    a little more, from founder cell to hatching (let's say

coffee, lots). And found
                              he had transcribed there? Found

                    that death was not an afterthought. The genome
                              is a river too. And simpler, far

                                                       more elegant, to

keep the single system and discard the extra cells
                                        it spawns. So *apo-*

(Gk., away from) *ptosis* (fall), as leaves

                              preserve the tree by learning
                    to relinquish it. A river
                                        of intelligence runs through us, could
          the part we do on purpose do

                              less harm. One version
of the lesson is its usefulness, the kindred
                              genes that help us break the circuit

                    of malignancy, we name them for what happens when
                              they fail.
                              But use is not

          the whole of it. *He wants* said my father (and this
                    of one he loved) *to live*

forever so I knew it was contemptible (had loved
    forever). Death
                is not an afterthought nor

        (mother of beauty) will death
                    undone assist us, we
are made of it, are cognate (mother) to the worm, a worthy

                      daily labor and this thread
        of in-the-cells remembering make it so.

Notes

Bicameral

Sections two and three are based on the work of the Polish artist Magdalena Abakanowicz (b. 1930) and on interviews published in Barbara Rose, *Magdalena Abakanowicz.* New York: Harry Abrams, 1994. The exhibit described in section three, "Atelier 72," was mounted at the Richard Demarco Gallery in Edinburgh, August 1972.

Make-Falcon

Frederick II of Hohenstaufen (1194–1250), Holy Roman Emperor, King of Sicily and Jerusalem. Student of mathematics, natural history, architecture, and philosophy. Crusader, falconer, poet. Founder of the University of Naples. Patron to Giacomo (also called Jacopo) da Lentino (fl. 1215–33), generally credited with the invention of the sonnet.

The Burning of Madrid as Seen from the Terrace of My House

Juan Muñoz, Spanish sculptor and installation artist (1953–2001), retrospective exhibition at the Art Institute of Chicago (September 14– December 8, 2002). For the catalogue, see Neal Benezra and Olga M. Viso, *Juan Muñoz.* Chicago: University of Chicago Press and the Art Institute of Chicago, 2001.

Father Mercy, Mother Tongue

"If the English language was good enough for Jesus Christ, it is good enough for the schoolchildren of Texas" — Miriam "Ma" Ferguson, governor of Texas, 1924–26.

At the Window

The *Confessions* of St. Augustine, Book IX, trans. R. S. Pine-Coffin.

The Turning

Ingmar Bergman, *Winter Light (Nattvardsgästerna),* 1962. Cinematographer, Sven Nyqvist (1922–2006).

De Magnete

I have taken considerable liberty with the language though not the substance of my sources, chief among them William Gilbert's great treatise *On the Magnet*. The Norwegian: Roald Amundsen, polar explorer.

Dido in Darkness

Christopher Marlowe's play as performed by Angels in the Architecture, at the Chapel of the House of St. Barnabas-in-Soho (London) in 2006.

Elegant

In 2002 the Nobel Prize in physiology was awarded to Sydney Brenner, Robert Horvitz, and John Sulston for discoveries concerning "genetic regulation of organ development and programmed cell death." *C. elegans* was the model organism used in their research. My thanks to Nelson Horseman for calling my attention to this beautiful work, to John Sulston for sharing with me the text of his Nobel lecture, and, above all, to Ron Ellis for his patient and generous tutelage.